CREATURES THAT
GLOW

ISBN 0–8109–4027–2
Library of Congress Catalog Card Number: 95–75213

Copyright © 1995 by Marshall Editions Developments Limited, London

Published in 1995 by Harry N. Abrams, Incorporated, New York
A Times Mirror Company

Creatures that Glow is a Marshall Edition

Marshall Editions would like to thank the following artists for illustrating this
book: *Obin* for pages 8–11, 14–17, 24–25, and the sea creatures on the poster;
Roger Stewart for pages 20–21, 26–29, and the rest of the images on the poster;
and *Peter Sarson* for pages 12–13, 18–19, 22–23.

Editor: *Steve Setford*
Designer: *Stephen Woosnam-Savage*
Managing Editor: *Kate Phelps*
Design Manager: *Ralph Pitchford*
Art Director: *Branka Surla*
Editorial Director: *Cynthia O'Brien*
Production: *Janice Storr, Angela Kew*

Printed and bound in Spain

CREATURES THAT
GLOW

Text by
Anita Ganeri

Introduction by
Dr. Peter Herring

Harry N. Abrams, Inc., Publishers

CONTENTS

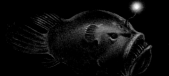

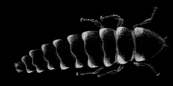

INTRODUCTION

Bioluminescence—light produced by living things—is a wonder of the natural world. Thousands of animals and plants in the sea and on land can glow or sparkle with their own light. They may live in places where there is little natural light, or come out only at dusk or when it is dark. Some animals use their light to signal one another or other creatures—whether to find a mate, to distract or frighten attackers, to camouflage themselves, or to illuminate their prey.

Most creatures that glow produce their own light by chemical reactions inside special light organs, although some have to eat luminous prey to get a supply of the right chemicals. A few glowing fish and squid cannot do this, but they can still sparkle because their light organs provide a home to luminous bacteria: when the bacteria glimmer, so does the creature itself. Just like traffic signals or flashlights, these light organs may have complicated lenses, reflectors, and color filters to make them work efficiently.

Deep in the ocean is a vast dark world where little light can penetrate. So it is not surprising that there are many more kinds of luminous creatures and plants living in the sea than on land. Very few of them have common names, but each species is given a unique Latin name which is recognized by all biologists, whatever their own language. Often these names include a word that describes the light ("*luminosa*," "*scintillans*," "*phosphorea*"). A tiny luminous plant, large numbers of which often make the sea shimmer, is called *Noctiluca scintillans*. Its name means "sparkling night light."

Although we cannot glow ourselves, we can marvel at the ingenuity of those creatures that can.

Dr. Peter Herring

ANGLER FISH

In the depths of the sea it is always pitch black because no sunlight can reach that far down. The deep-sea angler fish copes with the darkness by making its own light. It has a fin, like a long fishing rod, growing from its snout. At the end of the fin is a glowing light, or lure, that acts as bait to tempt prey into range of the angler fish's large, gaping mouth. Angler fish feed on small fish, squid, crustaceans, worms, and any other creatures they can catch. These creatures probably mistake the blob of light for a tasty snack.

Only the female angler fish has this amazing fishing rod. Males are much smaller and less bizarre in appearance. During mating, the tiny male attaches himself by his teeth to the female. His body then fuses into hers—all that is left of the male is a small pouch on the female's side. The pouch contains the male's reproductive organs, which will fertilize the female's eggs.

Linophryne arborifera

Deep-sea angler fish are dark brown or black in color. This camouflages them in the pitch-black water. Unlike many other fish, most angler fish do not have scales, although some have spiny or warty skin.

Many angler fish are slow, sluggish swimmers. They do not have streamlined bodies because they do not need to move swiftly to catch their prey. Some lie on the ocean bed, mouth agape, waiting for prey to be attracted by the glowing lure.

DEEP-SEA ANGLER FISH—
6 inches long (female)

Female deep-sea angler fish (*Melanocoetus johnsoni*)

Thaumatichthys
pagidostomus

Football fish
(*Himantolophus*
groenlandicus)

▲ *There are about 100 species*
of angler fish, ranging from
about 2½ to 35 inches in
length. The deepest-living are
found more than a mile down,
in warm, tropical seas. Other
species live in shallow water
along the coasts.

The fishing rod growing from
the deep-sea angler fish's
snout ends in a glowing blob
of light. It is made up of
millions of light-making
bacteria that give off a bluish
or greenish-yellow light.

The deep-sea angler fish has
a huge mouth, lined with
terrifying rows of long, curved
teeth. The teeth lie backward
to let prey into the fish's
mouth. Then they spring
back into place to stop
it from escaping again.

FIREFLY

On a summer's night, bright flashing lights can often be seen dancing through the air, lighting up trees, or shining out from the undergrowth. These are fireflies, also known as glowworms or lightning bugs. Despite their names, they are actually types of beetles. Fireflies are famous for their yellowish-green lights, which they produce through chemical reactions inside their bodies.

Fireflies flash their lights in the darkness to attract mates. Each species has its own pattern of flashes—a kind of "call sign" that allows fireflies of the same species to recognize one another. They use different lengths of flashes, long and short, and can change the frequency and brightness of their signals. In some species, it is the male who flashes first to attract the female, while in other species, the females do the "calling." Both the male and female die soon after they have mated.

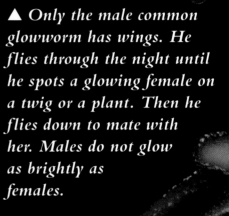

▲ *Only the male common glowworm has wings. He flies through the night until he spots a glowing female on a twig or a plant. Then he flies down to mate with her. Males do not glow as brightly as females.*

**FIREFLY
(Common glowworm)—**

Female
¼ inch

Male
⅜ inch

Shown at actual size

Some fireflies use their lights in self-defense. They flash to warn enemies that they taste nasty and should be left alone! Female fireflies stop producing light after they have mated.

◀ *In Southeast Asia, male fireflies gather in trees at dusk and flash their lights on and off in unison to attract females. There may be thousands of males in a single tree.*

1. Eggs   2. Larva   3. Pupa   4. Adult

LIFE CYCLE

After mating, the female lays her eggs under a stone or beneath vegetation. Five weeks later, the eggs hatch and larvae crawl out. They spend a year growing and feeding before pupating and turning into adults. A firefly glows at every stage of its life.

The female common glowworm cannot fly. At dusk, she crawls up a grass stem or twig and waves her glowing tail at the sky to attract a male. Her light organs are on the underside of her abdomen.

This firefly is known as the common glowworm (Lampyris noctiluca). It lives in forests, meadows, and marshes throughout Europe. Fireflies are found all over the world, although the majority of the 2,000 species live in warm, tropical countries. New species are being discovered all the time.

11

FLASHLIGHT FISH

When night falls, the flashlight fish emerges from its hiding place among rocks or in a coral reef. It is very wary of any light and will soon dart for cover if the moonlight is too bright, or if it catches a glimpse of a human diver's torch. In the safety of the darkness, flashlight fish use their own light to find their prey of plankton and tiny crustaceans, to confuse their enemies, and to communicate with each other. The bright light is produced by large organs under each eye. These contain millions of luminous bacteria that emit light as they are nourished by sugar and oxygen in the fish's blood.

The fish can blink their lights on and off, and swivel them around to help in their search for food. The beams of light they produce are so powerful they can be seen more than 100 feet away. In fact, the light from a single flashlight fish is bright enough to light up a small room.

Flashlight fish live in the shallow waters of the Indian and Pacific oceans. They are active only at night. Local people catch the fish, remove their still-glowing flashlights, and use them as fishing bait. The light organs will glow for several hours after the fish is dead.

Flashlight fish
(*Photoblepharon
palpebratus*)

**FLASHLIGHT FISH—
3¼ inches long**

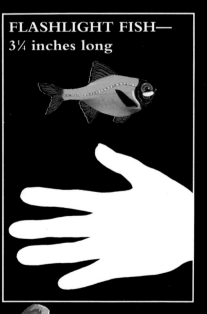

Flashlight fish have a light organ under each eye. They turn their lights on and off by raising or lowering shutters of dark skin like eyelids. The shutters' black lining prevents light from being seen when they are closed.

▲ If a flashlight fish is threatened by a predator, it turns its lights off, darts away, and suddenly flashes them on again elsewhere. It repeats this sequence on a mazelike, zigzagging escape route that confuses the attacker.

▼ Pine-cone fish produce light with the help of millions of bacteria in two light organs under their jaws. Pine-cone fish get their name from the armor of thick, overlapping scales that covers their bodies.

Pine-cone fish
(*Monocentris japonicus*)

Pony fish
(*Gazza minuta*)

◄ The pony fish's two bacteria-filled light glands are located at the back of its throat. The fish emits the light as flashes or a constant glow. It also grunts when threatened, to scare off attackers.

RAILROAD WORM

The railroad worm is not really a worm at all, but the wormlike adult female or the larva of the *Phrixothrix* beetle. *Phrixothrix* means "with bristling hairs" and refers to the covering of tiny hairs on its body. The railroad worm lives in South and Central America, where it is rarely seen because it is shy and nocturnal.

The railroad worm comes out at night to hunt for food. If it finds itself under threat, it suddenly switches on the bright lights on its head and body to warn the attacker to stay away. In this extraordinary display, its head glows a fiery red and its body a pale greenish-yellow. It also lights up when attacking other creatures and while mating. The lights are produced by a chemical reaction inside the railroad worm's body. By day, it is a different story. Railroad worms are normally a drab brown color that camouflages them as they hide away under logs or rocks, or under the ground.

On each side of its body the railroad worm has 11 spots of light that shine a pale greenish-yellow. A railroad worm can turn all its lights on at once, or just a few at a time. Only the female worm has the bright red light on its head as well.

Female adult railroad worm
(*Phrixothrix tiemanni*)

RAILROAD WORM—2½ inches long

Life-size adult female (males are about half the size of females)

A railroad worm hunts insects and millipedes to eat, often devouring prey much larger than itself. It glows as it curls around the body of its prey and kills it with a poisonous bite from its large, curved jaws. Railroad worms have even been known to eat other railroad worms.

The railroad worm gets its name because its glowing body-lights look like the windows of a night train, with a bright red headlight at the front.

LIFE CYCLE

The female lays a cluster of eggs in her underground burrow. She curls around them protectively until wormlike larvae hatch from the eggs. After about a year, the larvae turn into pupae. Adults emerge from the pupae less-than a month later. Only the male beetles have wings.

Male

Female

4. Adults emerge

3. Larvae turn into pupae

Male

Female

2. Larvae hatch from the eggs

1. Cluster of eggs

15

SEASTAR

Seastars belong to a group of creatures called echinoderms, which also includes sea urchins, sea cucumbers, brittlestars, and featherstars. Echinoderm means "spiny skinned," and most echinoderms are covered with sharp spikes for self-defense. Echinoderms live on the seashore, among coral reefs, and on the sea bed.

Some seastars, brittlestars, sea cucumbers, and featherstars produce their own light to warn off predators such as fish or crabs. They may have luminous arms or spines, or be able to pour clouds of light into the water when attacked.

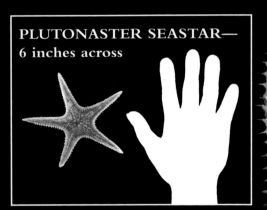

**PLUTONASTER SEASTAR—
6 inches across**

**Seastar
(*Plutonaster
notatus*)**

▲ *This brittlestar flashes brightly when attacked and may throw off the tip of one of its arms to distract the enemy. The tip continues to flash while the brittlestar escapes.*

▲ *This seastar lives on the sea bed about 3,300 feet down. It glows all over with a greenish-blue light, which is brightest at the tips of its five arms. It warns would-be predators that it has a nasty taste!*

1. Eggs are fertilized

2. Young larva

3. Mature larva

4. Young adult

LIFE CYCLE
The female seastar's eggs are fertilized in the water by the male. They develop into larvae that drift with the surface plankton before changing into bottom-dwelling adults.

FUNGI

Honey fungus
(*Armillaria mellea*)

Fungi are neither plants nor animals. They form the group of living things that includes mildews, molds, mushrooms, and toadstools. Fungi feed on living or dead matter, spreading a mass of tiny threads over their food and sucking out the nutrients. About 40 species of fungi, growing in woods and tropical forests, produce their own green or bluish-green light. Some have glowing bodies that light up at night. Others grow on branches and tree trunks, illuminating the bark or bare wood with their network of shining threads. Both types of fungi produce light by means of chemical reactions. No one is really certain why they do this.

▲ *The rootlike threads of the honey fungus glow as they burrow into wood. This fungus attacks tree trunks, stumps, and roots.*

Mycena toadstool

▶ *The luminous* Mycena *toadstool grows among the leaf litter of the forest floor in the jungles of Southeast Asia.*

Pleurotus lampus

▶ *This glowing fungus is found in Australia. At night it glows with an eerie white light, perhaps to attract insects to help disperse its spores, which rub off onto their wings and bodies.*

FUNGI range in size from tiny microscopic molds to vast growths such as *Armillaria bulbosa*, which develops a network of threads that may extend through the soil for several square miles.

FIREFLY SQUID

1. Adults mate

The firefly squid produces blue-white light chemically. Its body and tentacles are studded with jewel-like light organs. The squid can camouflage itself by altering the color, intensity, and angle of its lights to match its surroundings.

Japanese firefly squid
(*Watasenia scintillans*)

I n spring, Japanese fishermen haul in a very special catch that makes their nets glitter and sparkle with light. For this is when millions of firefly squid come to the surface to breed—and to be caught by the ton! It is thought that firefly squid produce light in order to attract a mate or to camouflage themselves. By matching the light coming from above, they can make themselves invisible to predators below them in the water. In Japan, firefly squid are eaten as a delicacy.

Some species of squid use light for self-defense. They can squirt out clouds of luminous mucus to confuse their enemies and give themselves time to escape. On the island of Madeira, fishermen bait their lines with pieces of luminous squid to attract fish.

Squid are strong, fast swimmers that jet-propel themselves along by pumping water in and out of their bodies. Some species can dart through the water at speeds of up to 25 miles an hour! A funnel-like opening allows them to direct the jet forward or backward.

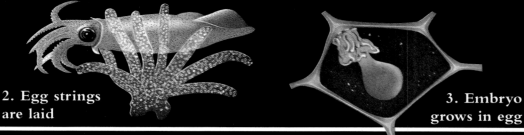

**2. Egg strings
are laid**

**3. Embryo
grows in egg**

**4. Baby squid
emerges**

LIFE CYCLE

*After mating, the female firefly squid lays soft strings of
eggs and attaches them to the sea floor. The eggs harden
and grow as the embryos develop inside. About 10 days
later, baby squid hatch out from the eggs.*

▼ *The deep-sea squid is
dotted all over with light
organs. They produce a
bright enough light to show
up on a photograph taken
in the dark without a flash.*

*Japanese firefly squid live some
1,000 feet down in the Pacific
Ocean off the coast of Japan.
They are about the length of a
human finger.*

**Deep-sea squid
(*Selenoteuthis
scintillans*)**

**JAPANESE FIREFLY SQUID—
2 inches long**

Shown at actual size

19

FUNGUS GNAT

Fungus gnats are tiny, flylike insects that live in caves, hollow trees, and other dark, damp places in New Zealand. They are best known for their glowing, wormlike larvae, which have developed an ingenious way of catching prey.

The nest of a fungus gnat larva is a transparent tube of mucus. From the tube hangs a curtain of silky threads up to 20 inches long, each covered in droplets of glue. The larva lies in its tube, waving its glowing tail to light up the threads. Midges, moths, and other insects are lured toward the shining curtain.

When an insect touches one of the threads, it is trapped by the sticky droplets. As it struggles to escape, vibrations run along the thread and alert the larva, which emerges from its tube. The larva pulls in the thread, like an angler hauling in a fish, and devours its catch.

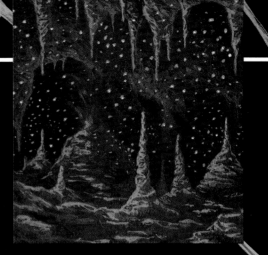

▲ *New Zealand's Waitomo Cave is famous as the home of millions of fungus gnat larvae. They live in tubes stuck to the cave ceiling, making it glitter like a sky full of stars.*

The tip of the larva's tail glows with light produced chemically inside its body. It shines its light onto its "fishing lines" to make them glimmer and shine in the darkness.

Fungus gnat larva
(*Arachnocampa luminosa*)

Up to 70 long threads hang from the larva's nest, ready to trap insects with their sticky coating. Adult fungus gnats may also get caught in the threads, but they usually manage to escape.

1. Eggs are laid

2. Larvae hatch

3. Pupae form

4. Adults emerge

LIFE CYCLE

The female lays about 130 eggs, often on the walls or ceiling of a cave. The larvae hatch and live for about a year before shedding their skins and turning into pupae. About 12 days later, the pupae split open and fully formed adults emerge, complete with wings and legs. The larvae, pupae, and adults all produce light. Only the eggs do not glow.

FUNGUS GNAT LARVA—
1 inch long

HATCHET FISH

Camouflage is vital to the hatchet fish because it is preyed upon by many larger fish. Its reflective, mirrorlike sides help to disguise it when viewed from the side.

The hatchet fish gets its name because its silvery body, sharp-edged belly, and slender tail make it look like an ax.

The hatchet fish has almost 100 light-producing organs on its underside that emit a bluish, downward-pointing glow.

Hatchet fish are small, shiny, silvery fish. They are found in all the world's oceans except the polar seas. In the dim daylight, they lurk at a depth of about 1,600 feet, but during the night, they swim within 1,000 feet of the surface to feed.

Hatchet fish are probably the best camouflaged of all ocean fish. Like many other deep-sea fish, they have lines of light-producing organs spread all along their undersides. Inside these organs, chemicals react together and give out a dim, pale blue light that matches the daylight around them and hides them from predators below. Each species of hatchet fish has its own particular pattern of lights.

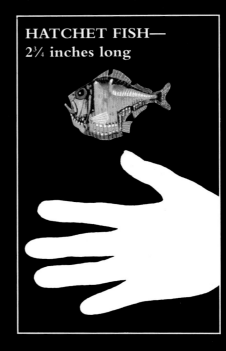

HATCHET FISH—
2¾ inches long

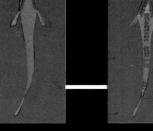

▲ *Most deep-sea predators search for prey in the water above them, recognizing their dark shapes against light filtering down from the surface. To avoid being seen and eaten, the hatchet fish's light organs break up its silhouette and make it difficult to spot from below.*

Hatchet fish feed on tiny crustaceans. They have large, upturned eyes and a wide, upturned mouth to locate and catch food drifting down from the water above.

Deep-sea hatchet fish
(*Argyropelecus aculeatus*)

MICROSCOPIC LIFE

The sea is swarming with billions and billions of tiny plants and animals called plankton. They form the start of the ocean food chain, and all animal life in the sea ultimately depends on them for survival. Most types of plankton are invisible, because they are too small to be seen with the naked eye. Some, however, let their presence be known by making their own light chemically. If a boat or a wave churns up the sea at night, the dark water suddenly sparkles and twinkles with light as if ablaze.

Among the luminous plankton are microscopic plants, called dinoflagellates, and tiny crustaceans, called copepods and ostracods, which are related to shrimp, crabs, and prawns. They all produce light if they are disturbed, possibly to warn off predators. Large numbers of dinoflagellates can make enough light to read by.

▶ **Peridinium divergens** *has a long, whiplike "tail" called a flagellum, which it thrashes from side to side to move itself through the water.*

Dinoflagellate
(*Peridinium divergens*)

▼ *Copepods drift in the upper waters of the sea, grazing on plant plankton. In turn, they provide a major source of food for fish and other larger animals.*

Copepod
(*Pleuromamma abdominalis*)

MICROSCOPIC LIFE—
Gymnodinium splendens
magnified 650 times (x 650)
Ceratium longipes x 800
Peridinium divergens x 700
Noctiluca scintillans x 200
Vargula hilgendorfi x 50
Pleuromamma abdominalis x 50

▶ **Noctiluca** *means "night light." These tiny dinoflagellates are found drifting in the open waters of warm seas. Dinoflagellates produce their blue-green light by means of chemicals inside their bodies.*

Dinoflagellate
(*Gymnodinium splendens*)

◄ *Dinoflagellates are single-celled sea plants that drift through the world's oceans, moving up to the surface waters to feed. Not all dinoflagellates are luminous, but they all have at least one flagellum, and many have strange shapes.*

► *Ostracods are tiny, bean-shaped crustaceans that use their bluish lights to attract a mate or deter predators. Some drift among the plankton, while others live near the sea bottom, feeding on plant and animal scraps.*

Ostracod
(*Vargula hilgendorfi*)

Dinoflagellate
(*Noctiluca scintillans*)

Dinoflagellate
(*Ceratium longipes*)

► *Dinoflagellates flash their lights if there are predators such as copepods nearby. These lights not only disturb the copepods, but they also work like burglar alarms, alerting fish and other large predators. When the fish arrive, they eat the copepods and remove the danger.*

25

DRAGONFISH

Black loosejaw
(*Malacosteus niger*)

It is easy to see how the dragonfish got its name. With its fearsome teeth, flashing lights, and the strange feeler dangling from its chin, it looks every inch like a deep-sea monster. Dragonfish produce their own light by means of chemical reactions inside their bodies. Females have light organs behind their eyes and along the sides of their long, streamlined bodies. The males are so unlike the females that they look like completely different fish. Males are much smaller than females, and they do not have barbels or teeth in their jaws, although they do have large light organs behind their eyes. They are also a different color—males are pale brown, while females are black or very dark brown with white fins. Females of the black dragonfish species may live for several breeding seasons, but males only live for a few weeks or months.

▲ *Other relations of the black dragonfish include loosejaws, viperfish, and scaled dragonfish. They all have light organs and sharp, bristlelike teeth. Most luminous deep-sea fish glow with bluish or bluish-green light. Loosejaws are unusual because they also have organs with a reddish glow.*

The black dragonfish has been found living in the depths of the Atlantic Ocean, eastern Indian Ocean, and western parts of the Pacific Ocean. It usually lives some 6,000 feet below the surface. During the day, it swims up toward the surface in search of food.

BLACK DRAGONFISH—
12–16 inches long (female)

Black dragonfish
(*Idiacanthus fasciola*)

Sloane's viperfish
(*Chauliodus sloani*)

Scaled dragonfish
(*Stomias boa*)

▼ *Dragonfish hatch from eggs and then go through a series of remarkable changes. Before turning into adults, they grow into transparent larvae, whose eyes stick out from their bodies on long stalks.*

Dragonfish larva

A female dragonfish has a large light organ behind each eye and rows of small light organs along her sides. Her fins and tail are also lined with light-producing cells.

Young female

Adolescent female

The female dragonfish has a long, luminous feeler, called a barbel, dangling from her chin. Dragonfish may use their barbels as lures to tempt prey toward their open mouths.

Dragonfish larvae feed on plankton and crustaceans. Adult females eat small fish. Their strong, gaping jaws bristle with long, sharp teeth to prevent prey from slipping out of their grasp. It is thought that the males do not feed once they are fully grown.

27

Comb Jelly

Beroe

Comb jellies are delicate sea creatures with many of the same features as jellyfish and sea anemones. They range in size from just one-fifth of an inch to more than three feet in length. Comb jellies feed mainly on tiny sea animals and plants called plankton. Some catch their prey with sticky tentacles that they trail through the water like fishing lines. Others have a very "elastic" mouth that stretches wide open to engulf their prey— including other comb jellies!

A comb jelly has rows of tiny hairs, or cilia, that look like minute combs. The jelly moves the cilia to propel itself through the water. Almost all comb jellies have special light-producing cells along the seamlike ridges of their bodies. To startle predators and drive them away, comb jellies give a spectacular display of flashing lights at the slightest contact.

▲ *There are about 100 species of comb jellies. This one has no tentacles, but swims along mouth first, catching food as it travels. Most jellies have colorless or very pale transparent bodies, although a few are purple or red.*

The football-sized red comb jelly flashes when touched. It also pours sparkling luminous particles into the water from its comb rows.

RED COMB JELLY—
10–12 inches long

Red comb jelly

Lampea

▲ *This comb jelly has a white, coiled tentacle loaded with sticky cells. The cells catch drifting food items as the jelly hovers in the water. To eat the food, the jelly retracts the tentacle and draws it across its mouth. This Lampea is eating salps, types of plankton, which can be seen inside its transparent body.*

Comb jellies are so delicate that they are almost impossible to catch in nets without destroying them. Some, such as this splendid red comb jelly, are only discovered because they are seen by scientists exploring the deep ocean. The red comb jelly lives in the Caribbean at depths of 2,000 to 3,000 feet.

▼ *The comb jelly below is called a sea gooseberry because of its round, "hairy" body. It lives in the Atlantic and Pacific oceans, often in large groups. The sea gooseberry's tentacles extend up to 20 inches from its body.*

Sea gooseberry
(*Pleurobrachia*)

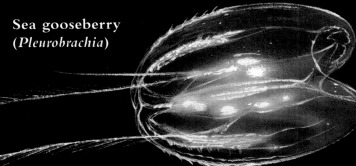

GLOSSARY

Bacteria
Microscopic, single-celled organisms that are found almost everywhere. Some produce light, while some others can cause diseases.

Barbel
A long, thin feeler, sometimes found around a fish's mouth.

Camouflage
Color or pattern on an animal's body that helps it to hide in its surroundings and so be concealed from enemies.

Crustacean
Crustaceans are creatures that have external skeletons and live mainly in the sea. They include crabs, shrimp, lobsters, and barnacles.

Fertilize
When a male sex cell joins with a female sex cell to make a new plant or animal.

Gland
An organ in the body which produces special substances, such as chemicals, that are used in other parts of the body.

Larva (plural: larvae)
The young form of an animal, such as an insect, which looks very different from the adult. For example, beetles and flies have grublike larvae.

Luminous
Something that produces or emits light.

Mate
Male and female animals mate with each other in order to produce young.

Mucus
A slimy, sticky substance.

Nocturnal
An animal that is active at night, when it comes out to look for food. Badgers, bats, and owls are nocturnal.

Organ
Part of a creature's body that has a specific job to do.

Plankton
Tiny plants and animals that float within the sea.

Predator
An animal that hunts and kills other animals for food.

Prey
Animals that are hunted or killed by other animals for food.

Pupa (plural: pupae)
The stage in the life of many insects between larva and adult. The larva spins a silken cocoon around itself. Inside the cocoon, its body changes into an adult.

Spore
A tiny, seedlike speck that can grow into a new plant or fungus.

INDEX